The Wolf
Entrepreneurial Fundamentals

Walk into the wilderness prepared. Have an attack plan when moving in on the kill. Make no mistake about it you're in the fight for your life. To truly attack and win you will need to be sharp, keen, and laser focused. Once you make your presence known you will be flanked and killed before you know what hit you.

The lion is the king of the jungle and nobody fucks with the lion. When a wolf and his pack are hungry enough the lion is no match from a stealthy hunting pack of wolves. It's the law of the jungle, kill or be killed. Patience and a keen sense will prevail. Rushing in for the kill because you're starving will only get you hurt. Develop your fundamentals and surround yourself with a pack of wolves that are just as keen and patient as you

This book is dedicated to my children. May you always have the courage to brave the wilderness, be authentic, ask for advice, and never never get up.

The Fundamental List

1. Functionally Fit
2. Fuel Your Machine
3. Stop Sleepwalking
4. Take Action
5. Become Laser Focused
6. Positive People
7. Leadership
8. Play
9. Be Adventurous
10. Boxing Yourself In
11. Be Vulnerable
12. Gossip
13. Forgive Yourself
14. Listen Intently
15. Don't Procrastinate
16. Fail Daily
17. Think Success
18. Be Authentic
19. Break Addictions
20. Sell Sell Sell
21. Schedule, It
22. Going Big'
23. Business Planning
24. Write it Down
25. Be The Wolf

Sean P Duron

1. **Functionally Fit.**

You might be asking yourself what the hell does being functionally fit have anything to do with my success as an entrepreneur? Everything. First, it gives you confidence knowing that you look good, feel good, and have the strength to get through the day kicking ass. Being functionally fit will help keep you balanced, focused, and ready to attack when the moment presents itself.

The stress we endure as entrepreneurs wreaks havoc on our systems, so we must protect it by being functionally fit will all life throws at us. The wolf and his pack must endure the cold winter months, scarce food supply, and fighting off other wolf packs. This is exactly what entrepreneurs endure and it's why we must have the energy, flexibility, and strength to handle the stresses we undergo.

Being functionally fit will allow you to breathe deeper, sleep harder and more sound, allowing you to fall into the rem sleep needed for recovery of your brain, muscles, and various systems of the body. You'll have more energy to get more done throughout the day and into the night.

The older we get the more our bodies will break down, bones become weak, increased likelihood of cancer, heart disease, Alzheimer's disease, dementia, COPD, and an array of other diseases we can fight off through a functionally fit lifestyle. Live to grow old and enjoy your successes, your children, and your grandchildren. Become functionally fit at www.corejungle.com

2. **Fuel Your Machine**

Diets are bullshit. They don't work. Eat realistically for a lifestyle that promotes good health. If you owned a Ferrari are you going to put crappy gas in it? You can for a short while, but the engine and its systems will prematurely fail and now you have a shiny car that goes nowhere. Is that where you want to go in life...nowhere? When a wolf goes too long eating field mice and scraps found from wherever he will become weak, slow, and lose focus. Eventually he will be attacked and eaten.

Enough excuses of why you don't eat right. As soon as you make excuses for one thing in your life it becomes a domino effect for other walks in life. The hell with field mice, eat what the lions are eating and become strong internally as well as externally.

For further information about nutrition click here: www.corejungle.com

3. **Stop Sleepwalking**

Open your eyes to a world of unlimited possibilities. Don't be a sheep. Don't follow trends. Be the trendsetter by being authentic and new. Have imagination and let your creativity soar. Don't be the wolf that gets caught in the snare. Live in Awareness; see behind you without turning around. See the big picture while focusing on the microscopic details.

Know your purpose, your passion and walk with a purpose, speak with a purpose, and listen intently. Stop meandering and search your soul for the real you. Know what your principles are and stand firm but be flexible in your business. Know your worth but be humble and have gratitude and never, never, never give up in the face of adversity.

4. Take Action

Don't procrastinate just get the damn thing started. Call it a test run or practice, but don't try and be perfect your first time out. Just go for it and fail every day, learn by doing, understand the stones you stumbled on as not to stumble on the same stones twice. Face your fear head on don't be scared to go for it each day. Make progress with a planned goal of where you will be at the end of each day. Take each day as it comes and don't worry about tomorrow and let yesterday's failures belong to history.

It takes a very keen and experienced pack of wolves to hunt big game, so start fine-tuning your skills with small game. Don't let your perfectionism get in the way of progress. Get it 80% and then fine-tune it. Delegate authority and don't micro manage, allow the pack to feel the pride of "making it theirs" as well. Allow your team to "take ownership" and feel like they just aren't part of the team, but part of the product.

Take educated risk and don't attack without a plan. You must attack to win, so set a plan and go for it, but remember, no attack ever goes as planned. Lastly, keep it simple stupid.

5. **Become Laser Focused**

Don't just attack, attack methodically, aim small miss small. If you're a wolf attacking your prey focus on a single hair rather than the whole neck. Become laser focused on your daily goals and practice patience. Set timelines with each goal or your goal will just stay a dream.

Have meetings for the specific reason of checking timelines for each goal or setting new goals with timelines. Keep meetings short and sweet, follow up on each goal and don't get ahead of yourself. Remember to focus on the eye of the needle, not the shaft, point, width, or length, you're working on the eye of the needle until it's done, then move on from there.

When it's dead of winter and the wolf is at eat or be eaten time of his life, he will never be more laser focused and in the moment than right now.

"When you want success as bad as you want to breathe then you'll be successful" -Eric Thomas

6. **Positive People**

Nothing worse than a member of the pack that has questionable integrity, lack of drive, and promotes negative vibes within the business. That member should be removed immediately whether a friend or family member or not. Misery Loves Company so don't allow this type of character in the pack. One bad member can cause the entire team to fail big.

Positive people release positive energy, positive vibes that are contagious. I truly believe we are connected and we can literally feel the exuberance coming off positive people. When they walk into a room it's like they are glowing, because they are. Drop the negativity from your life befriend those you truly want to surround yourself with.

7. **Leadership**

As the lead wolf never ask anyone to do something you haven't done yourself or willing to do. You're never too above the employee that cleans the shitter and that's no lie. If something needs to be cleaned, clean it. Never be afraid to get into the fight and get a little bloody. Show the team through action that you're passionate about the product and business and willing to do whatever it takes to succeed morally and with a clean conscience.

Listen to your team first, don't speak, don't nod, just listen intently and be the last to speak. Man made the hierarchy, but a true leader sees no pyramid, no head of table, but as an equal within the team. He has the ability to motivate, delegate, and support his team with whatever they need. The leader makes sure they provide the tools and skills the team needs to complete goals on time.

A Leader knows how to inspire the team and the consumer, not by lowering prices, flashy packages, or money prizes, but truly inspire because they're authentic. Build relationships know your team, their families, desires, and their dreams. Be open and portray an open-door policy with absolutely no strings attached.

8. Play

Remember to be a kid and play without any remorse, guilt, or shame. Make a list of what truly brings you happiness that involves an activity and go do it. Take time out to play once a week at least. Drop all the bullshit, toss your cell phone in a drawer and get out for an entire afternoon and just have fun.

We all need to "dump the trash" at some point or it will overflow, and shit will start to build up...then it runs downhill. Next thing you know your team is covered in it.

Never forget to smile, laugh hard where your belly hurts and always have fun. When you try to be cool and act some way you think you should because of the environment, you're not having fun anymore, you're being what they want you to be. Be you, smile often and embrace the misery of entrepreneurship. It's just what we are it's what we do.

9. Be Adventurous

Have the courage to see what's on the other side of the mountain. Go down into the valley with guts to rise up on the mountain of glory. Push your limits as often as possible, don't let opportunities sneak by and go unchallenged. Do not allow yourself to become stagnant and comfortable. You have a responsibility to your team be creative, come up with new concepts, ideas, and products.

Being adventurous opens your endorphins and allows your mind to expand into new territories. Pushing yourself to the edge releases dopamine, which can allow us to stay stimulated mentally and physically. If you truly want to use all the tools that can help you become successful and stay there, pushing the limits and being adventurous is one of them.

Try new things constantly, don't let embarrassment stop you from experiencing all life has to offer. Take classes in self-defense, rock climbing, mountaineering, sailing, or whatever stirs your soul. Great entrepreneurs are risk takers, but they aren't stupid, they take calculated risks and listen to their gut.

10. Boxing Yourself In

Break the programming. Don't allow your parents, grandparents, teachers, church, or society program you into thinking a particular way. Be the renegade and do it your way. It may not have worked for others, but it may work well for you. Times change, society changes, so listen to your gut and go for it.

A wolf can't hide in her cave and protect her young forever. She needs to get out in the wilderness, find the water sources, best routes of travel, avoid other predators, and develop a keen sense. In addition, she must teach her young to brave the same.

You will succeed by getting out there and braving the wilderness of entrepreneurship yourself. Will you fail? Hell to the yes you will. In fact, you will fail so many times you'll question yourself time and time again. This is where your support team comes in and tells you that you will make it because they won't allow you to quit. You're a wolf not some sheep don't live mediocre don't accept to just survive but thrive and live well.

11. Be Vulnerable

This will be the hardest thing you'll most likely have to endure if you have the courage. It's about dropping your armor that we all put on each day. We go to work and put on a coat that is someone other than who we really are. We put on a coat of armor that is what we think we should be in that environment. We protect ourselves from being embarrassed, shamed, or just uncomfortable.

I hated hearing this the first time. It hit home for me harder than anything else that I ever read or heard. It was something I knew I needed to fix as soon as possible. I didn't want to live like that anymore, so I promised myself I would set a goal with a timeline to be authentic and real.

Seek and find for yourself through books, podcast, and meditation what it will take for you to drop the armor and become truly authentic and vulnerable.

12. Gossip

Stop the gossip within the business because it's cancer. It intertwines itself within the business and destroys morale, positive energy, and creates hate and discontent. Stop looking for confirmation that you aren't good enough because you'll always find it. Nip gossip in the bud as soon as it sprouts its ugly head.

People with low self-esteem talk about others negatively to make themselves feel better and if they can get you to agree all the better. Do you think a wolf has time for bullshit? Hell no, he's busy staying laser focused on what's best for the pack. He keeps his wit sharp and always ready to act. He knows if he lets his guard down for a second he'll lose the upper hand and could be compromised by other predators. Be the Wolf.

13. Forgive Yourself

God may have forgiven you, but have you forgiven yourself? Have you asked others for forgiveness? Let go of the guilt. Cry if you need to, cry hard and let it out. Let it go and breathe a sigh of relief. Open your heart, dump the hurt, the hate, and rejoice. Smile at yourself in the mirror and truly love wholeheartedly.

You're always going to have enemies and those that are jealous. You'll have people think your ideas and products don't do what you claim. Don't allow hate to build when this happens. Sure, you will feel upset, pissed off, hurt, and may even question yourself, but let those thoughts and feelings come in, accept them and let it go. Don't give your enemies good or bad because you're now giving them energy to pull you this way or that.

As you forgive yourself and let yourself be vulnerable people will see the real you. You'll be authentic, and people love that. People buy into you mostly, not just the product or idea. Have the courage to love your neighbor it's so much easier than revenge and hate. Hate will consume your progress and in the end, you'll be left all alone.

"The spirit of forgiveness is far better than the spirit of revenge." - Richard Branson.

14. Listen Intently

If you have something meaningful to say wait till everyone has spoken before speaking. Speak slow and annunciated, say it with purpose and conviction, otherwise, people won't truly listen. When you listen, listen with a purpose. Look at who you're speaking with, give them your undivided attention, put your cell phone in your pocket and leave it there. When you listen ask a question at the end rather than preparing your statement as soon as they finish speaking.

Learn to enjoy conversation, meeting others, and hearing their stories. Work alongside your team, your employees and listen to concerns and frustrations. Listen to your customers and be flexible in your marketing and product development.

15. Don't Procrastinate

Just go for it! Always be ready and willing to seize the moment! Don't worry if it's not perfect just get it 80% and fine tune the 20% later. Continue to make progress daily this is where the goals with timelines come into play. There are many businesses that put an offer out about their product, sell hundreds of them in a pre-sale, and never even made one. Sell, sell, sell, see it's sellable, marketable, and if it truly solves a problem people will buy. You'll never know until you try. The wolf will starve if he procrastinates too long, he must attack and go for it if he is to even have a chance.

16. Fail Daily

Failing is only failure if you quit. That's why we will claw our way even if our legs were caught in a trap. If you somehow knew you would have to fail 86 times before you made it would you quit at 40, 50 or 60? Of course not, you'd be thrilled you're getting closer to 87. You will succeed, just don't quit on yourself, your dreams, or your passion. Don't allow "life" to get in the way, don't become lazy, give in, and allow yourself to shelf your dreams.

17. Think Success

Truly successful people will already start acting like they're successful, walking confident, remain calm during stressful situations, and speak last. They'll start learning about themselves, learning to become balanced and in control. Don't wait till you succeed to change, work on it immediately. Believe in yourself, know you're successful at this very moment because you have the guts to go for it. You personally haven't seen the large checkbook or a product flying off the shelves, but you're living the dream! You're already winning!

Acting successful doesn't mean purchasing a flashy watch, new suit, and acting arrogant. It's becoming authentic, real, and mature. It's about putting the beer down, skipping the football game, the nachos, and partying lifestyle. It's about rolling your sleeves up and getting to work on you, your product, your ideas, and your dreams.

When you do start to see the big paychecks coming in don't throw your money out the window partying at clubs and showing off. Reinvest that money in you, your business, and your product to clear the next storm, because the storms will continue to come. As you build your shelter year after year, the storms won't affect you as bad. The older the wolf gets the wiser she gets because she invests in her future. She lives in the moment focused and aware, but is always preparing for the next winter.

18. Be Authentic

To become authentic will take work. It will be painful and nerve racking. You'll think of all those skeletons in your closet and every fault you have. That's good. Break bad habits and get to know who you truly are. Fix the shit you don't like about yourself and accept that you're only human like the rest of us.

Have you gossiped, talked shit, backstabbed, lied, or cheated? So what, we all do. Accept it all and move on. That's not you today, today you're making history and that past life belongs to history now. You need to embrace your wrong doings and take baby steps in fixing what you don't like about yourself to become truly authentic.

Read books, listen to audiobooks on self-development, read about other successful entrepreneurs, go to seminars, seek a counselor for help, and develop true character. Start understanding what your true principles are and stand firm. Ask yourself thought provoking questions that you may someday need to answer. Know why you stand for those principles with sincerity.

19. Break Addictions

Social media, alcohol, drugs, gambling, and pornography provides us with our "dopamine dose" and the addiction is real. Break the addiction and learn to have patience. Wait for true success to come along and see what a real high is all about. Don't give in to feeding the "I want it now" addiction, practice patience and surround yourself with those that are like-minded. Hold each other accountable. Stay committed to succeeding even if it takes years. Don't fall for instant gratifications learn to suffer. Don't find excuses to quit when it gets painful remember how bad you want it and see yourself winning.

20. Sell, Sell, Sell

Become a salesman first, learn your niche, your customers, and your selling strategy. Be authentic in your approach and build relationships with customers. The customer is always right, but are you truly focused on building the relationship or just getting them to buy?

Is it easier to keep your friends you have on a daily basis or go out each day and try to find new friends? Of course, it's much easier to keep friends, but as you continue to travel, get out and meet new people you'll continue to build new relationships. Look at customers or clients as a real relationship rather than a target.

Be careful getting advice from too many salespeople. Ask for advice from salespeople that you look up to, not just because they are bringing in lots of money. You can be a sleazy salesperson and still make shit loads of money, but that's not a road you want to go down. Be a person of value be authentic, and personal. Know the importance of people and branding yourself and your business. Sleep with a clear conscience; don't do something stupid when your back is against the wall because this is where you'll truly be tested as an entrepreneur.

21. Schedule, It

Being your own boss as an entrepreneur is one big reason you chose the lifestyle, but it comes with great responsibility, commitment, and self-drive. Schedule your day and week realistically and stick to it. You'll need to hold yourself accountable each day, saying no when you need to and know how to keep from getting caught up in a project or conversation that goes too long.

Schedule your time for workouts, preparing meals, meetings, answering emails, family time, and time for research, time for clients, etc. There will be days when shit happens and the whole day goes to hell, that's okay, deal with it and get back on track the next day. Set alarms on your phone to help keep you on track. Use technology to your advantage.

"I can tell how much money you make by looking at how you respect your time" -Mike Litman

22. Going Big

You want to hit the ground running hard, laser focused, and driven but hone your skills in on small game. When you and your team attacks, pick a single product that you believe will sell well and move onto the next product. You may have several products and ideas and that's fantastic, but remember to take baby steps, be patient, and laser focused on the eye of the needle. You can quickly become overwhelmed running into a herd of savory tempting prey, especially when you're hungry but you'll most likely become exhausted and running in circles.

You want to become a business with multiple products and services but remember to start off keeping it simple. That's one reason it takes years to develop real income. So, you need to go in with a business plan and cash flow to support a three-year or more plan. How will you continue to meet your overhead each month? Educate yourself in startup businesses similar to yours talk with business owners to get a much better idea of what lies ahead. Watch YouTube videos on start-ups, read books, and even take a college course on small business startups while you're saving up money to start your business.

23. Business Planning

Writing your business plan will be one of the most important and smart decisions you'll make. Nowadays, you can find all sorts of great information on writing a business plan on the Internet. I grew up in an era without computers and have seen the power in technology and education because of it. I had to go to the library and search for hours on a subject of interest or ask family and friends. Now I can usually find what I need to know from YouTube and Google searches. Be careful though, find reputable sources for your information, read reviews, look at how many followers they have and listen to your gut.

A business plan is exactly that, a plan. Your business plan is a living organic plan that will continue to change throughout the life of your business, so don't just write one and shelf it. Use your business plan like soldiers use a battle plan, follow the plan and be ready for every plan goes to hell when the attack is on. Be flexible and act rather than re-act because you know shit happens and you'll have to make some decisions on the fly.

Be patient and stick with it, you'll have some hurdles to overcome when writing your business plan, ask for advice, keep researching, and succeed. It will be a good test to see if you're resourceful enough and driven enough to be an entrepreneur. As an entrepreneur you'll need to be very resourceful, learn fast, and network, learn your strengths and weaknesses, and continue to learn the cycle of your business.

Even if you're not ready to start your business, research other businesses similar to yours in your area, conduct a demographic research, keep your ears and eyes open within your community. Go talk to the owners of the businesses, go in as a customer and see what you would do better. See what they offer, how they sell, market, and run the daily business. Talk to employees nonchalantly about their job, their likes and dislikes. Get in and get to know the community, the pricing, the good, the bad, and the ugly.

Get involved with the community, attend city and county meetings, get to know representatives, major players within your community and rub elbows with the suits of the town. Shake hands and introduce yourself, let people know you're there and you're interested in what's going on. You may even be able to help out with some non-profit organizations in your area. You never know who you'll meet and where those contacts can help down the line.

24. Write it Down

I know it's 2017 but there still is a thing called a notebook and pen that people use to write words down on something called paper. I actually wrote and mailed letters to family that took a week or more to receive because my dad wouldn't allow me to use the phone for long distance unless someone had died.

Keep a small notebook and pen with you as an entrepreneur. Write down thoughts, names, dates, ideas, quotes, and anything else you may need to reference later. Yea, you can just text it to yourself or speak into your voice memo on your smartphone, but writing it down helps put it into that thick skull of yours to remember. Plus, you should keep hard copies of names, dates, and ideas incase cyberspace loses your info.

When you do keep notebooks full of your ideas, dates of important milestones, etc., you'll be able to write your autobiography much easier and tell the world all the amazing things you accomplished as you grew into a successful entrepreneur.

25. Be The Wolf

You wake up each morning with a choice to be a wolf or a sheep. Will you be eaten, or will you attack? You must attack to win, act rather than re-act and always be ready. To be the leader of the pack takes growth in many areas within your life. You'll never stop learning or growing to continue your success as a person of true value.

Take a self-defense class to build your confidence. Learn to put yourself out in front because you know where you stand in your principles and you can make calculated decisions on the fly. Don't be afraid to take risks but don't lead your team in blind either.

Be centered and balanced and stick to a routine that allows you to get in your functional workouts, family time, play time, eating nutritiously, and meditate.

Never allow yourself to hit the snooze button remember you're living your dream and have goals to accomplish daily. Get out of bed, conduct some morning dynamic stretches, blast some music and set up your home for success.

Don't spread yourself too thin, tell people no and keep your eye on the target each day. The lead wolf has no time for bullshit or anything that doesn't help the success and progress of the business. Time is money and we fight for both every day.

Keep it simple and just be yourself, don't try and overthink shit. If you find yourself lost and getting frustrated take a break and breathe.

Keep meetings short and to the point. Have meetings to ensure goals and timelines are being met, get in and get out there's no need for a specific amount of time to lapse for a meeting to end.

If you need to get on the internet for something don't get lost surfing the net, checking Facebook, Instagram, or YouTube. Get your info and go!

When you push your idea or product out on the market try selling with one strategy, if it's not working try a different strategy. Don't become so passionate about one marketing strategy that you won't let go.

Set alarms on your phone to remind you to breathe and smile, be grateful for all you have and even send a quick text to a loved one letting them know how awesome they are.

Know your place, help those in need, remove gossip from your vocabulary, be authentic and promote positive energy. Surround yourself with like-minded nut cases like yourself. Just make sure they're smarter than you are.

I hope you take this little bit of advice and run with it, may it spark your soul to dive deeper into each topic and beyond. There is so much to learn, see, and discover out there technology is ever-changing and with it comes unlimited possibilities. Hit me up if you have questions or just want to check out my website. Thank you so much for taking the time to read this book, all the best in your adventures.

Sean P Duron

seandconsultant@gmail.com

www.corejungle.com

www.ingramcontent.com/pod-product-compliance
Lightning Source LLC
Chambersburg PA
CBHW031600210526
45464CB00003B/1363